Dedications

To all the turtles, actual and embodied,
not for the things they carry
or cannot escape, but for the ways they
remain stubbornly themselves;
to my dad for plotting with me
on my many schemes;
and to Mark for putting
silly thoughts in my head.
~A.R.G.

I dedicate this book to my daughter Amanda,
for inspiring me to collaborate with her
in illustrating this book, may the wonderful
worlds she creates through her writing
bring joy to children everywhere. I also
dedicate this book to all of my grandkids,
may you find the unique purpose
for which God created you.
~V.J.S.

Sir Frederique von Turtlestein

BY AMANDA GEERS

ILLUSTRATIONS BY VINCENT STEVENS

Evely & Vivian,
May you know your
strength that allows
you to defeat all
manner of dragons.
Amanda Geers

Sir Frederique von Turtlestein

BY **A**MANDA **G**EERS

ILLUSTRATIONS BY **V**INCENT **S**TEVENS

Contents

1

The Pond

On the island of San Juan, in the Royal Kingdom of the Ponds, there lived a brave young turtle, a Sir Frederique von Turtlestein.

The world above was a wondrous place.

There were farms with rows and rows of lavender that loved to mock the movements of the wind. There were mountains that slept in the background like tired giants with dandruff-capped hair.

But to think that there was a time when Frederique was not so brave and had never seen such wonders!

His brothers and sisters had learned from the harbor seals to lounge on warm rocks on sunny days. They had witnessed the shadow of the bald eagle and the stilted dance of the heron.

But Frederique had only known the bottom of Turtlestein Pond where he burrowed himself. He felt only the sludge of the mud, and the water was murky and dark.

With each passing season, he thought: *This is all of life there is for me. My brothers and sisters have light shells and can easily travel the land. But my shell is much larger and much heavier, it weighs me down, it slows me down. So it is much easier for me to settle here in the bottom of the pond.*

But in rare moments, he would admit to himself that he was incredibly lonely. For at the bottom, there was no one but the passing fish who stared at him side-eyed. Deep down beneath the hard layers of his shell, he wished he was "normal".

He wished he had some friends.

2

The Catfish and the Giant

One day as Frederique combed the mud for some plants, he felt a disturbance in the water that rippled from above. He peered upwards and saw a Catfish of the Royal Court thrashing on the surface.

"Dear me, help!" cried the catfish, caught on a fisherman's line. "What a tragedy! Someone, something, anything, save me from my undoing!"

Unable to completely ignore such a plea for help, Frederique swam up into the light-waters, past the struggling catfish, until he was in the shallow. He poked his head above the water, stretched forward, and chomped on the fisherman's bare big toe.

"Yeouch!" yelled the fisherman. Frederique now had just enough time to remove the hook and release the still bellowing catfish.

Once all seemed well, Frederique began his descent down to his more predictable and therefore, safe, monotony of mud.

"A moment please!" called the catfish. He caught up to Frederique and beamed, "I am absolutely grateful for your lifesaving efforts. That was brave indeed. I could have never challenged such a giant."

"It was nothing," mumbled Frederique. Though secretly, he was quite amazed by his actions as well.

"Brave, indeed. You know, maybe you could be just the one to defeat that terrible Dragon," said the catfish.

"What? What dragon?" asked Frederique.

"You haven't heard! Every night the Dragon races along the Dried River looking for his next meal. His eyes glow with a fire that pierces the night, and smoke billows from his mouth in angry spurts. He shows no mercy. Every clan has been affected: Seymour Snake's sister, Issabella; Patty, the beaver; and even some of your fellow Turtle clan."

"Well, yes, that sounds dreadful and quite depressing, yet another reason to return to the mud. I really must be going now," said Frederique.

"But you! You defeated a giant! And with one fell chomp! He could have easily crushed your head with his foot. Surely, if anyone has a chance," the catfish continued.

"Sorry," Frederique interrupted, "but I'm not the creature you're looking for, far from it actually."

"Hmmph. Well, I guess not then. But if it makes any difference, King Heron is offering a reward for such a daring endeavor. Allow me to quote his majesty: "To the creature courageous enough to defeat the Dragon of the Dried River, I will grant any favor of their choosing."

"Any favor?" said Frederique.

Perhaps, he thought, *King Heron in all his wisdom could give me a lighter shell; life wouldn't be so difficult for me then.*

3

The Storm

The catfish and giant were long gone now. Frederique remained all alone, uncertain and not quite ready to return to the gloom below.

A great storm was settling over the pond. A thunderstorm. The kind when the air is warm and heavy, and the clouds are large and angry.

Suddenly, lightning sprang!

The sky crashed like a ship ramming into a rocky shore. Soon the pond was overflowing, scattering turtles and crayfish, tadpoles and fry; sweeping all the animals past the reeds of the grassy marsh into standing water on the forest floor.

Very unwillingly far from home now, Frederique slowly adjusted to the sopping night, and through the downpour, he saw the tiniest bird. She was struggling under the weight of the mud and her drenched feathers. Such a small creature already, and what strength she had seemed to be fast plummeting.

Frederique was one accustomed to the mud and the way it keeps all exactly where it settles. He slid toward the bird on the smooth bottom of his shell. The bird was still. Frederique stretched his neck forward and lowered his head, lifted her on top, and let her roll down to rest on the back of his large and cumbersome shell.

4

Ruthie the Ruthless

It was late afternoon the next day when the tiny bird finally awoke.

Earlier that morning, Frederique, muddled and exhausted, had found the perfect rock to rest upon out on the edge of the forest. Frederique had never basked before; always too embarrassed to join the other turtles on the sunning logs, fearful his weighty shell would tip them all over. What a delight it was to bask and not cower! So much so, that he had stayed like that, like a perfect stone statue for hours.

During this time, the bird had lain in the sun, and the sun had dried the mud on her feathers. When she awoke, she ruffled her wings and the mud shook off her body like dust.

"Who are you? Who are you!" she twittled; buzzing around Frederique. Startled, Frederique nearly fell off his rock.

"I, I'm Frederique."

"A name is all the same. What, what, are you?"

"A turtle. I suppose I don't look it though. And you? I've never seen a bird like you, only the occasional diving duck," said Frederique.

"I'm no duck. I'm exotic, a bird from down south, a rufous hummingbird."

"And your name?" asked Frederique.

"Ruthie. But I'm known by most

as 'Ruthless.'"

"Oh! That's quite a serious nickname, even a bit terrifying," said Frederique. Though he questioned how much terror such a miniscule bird could cause.

"Quite right! I'm lightning fast and a relentless fencer. That's why I've flown all this way--to slay the infamous Dragon of the Dried River."

Suddenly, Ruthie the Ruthless fell from where she had been hovering and landed with a soft thud. She lay on the ground looking away and let out a discouraged sigh. She was still exhausted from her long journey and her struggles in the storm.

"I, too, have an interest in defeating the Dragon," said Frederique. "But in truth, I don't know what I'm doing or where I am going. Perhaps we could team up, and I can carry you on my shell whenever you are feeling tired or the weather is bad."

Frederique continued, "I'll help you get to the Dried River to defeat the Dragon. If only you persuade King Heron to grant me a favor as well, for I wish terribly to have a new, smaller and much lighter shell."

"Fine," the little bird said, "a favor for you and fame for me."

5

A Safe Escape

The following days, Ruthie steadily recovered and became just a blur of feathers dashing ahead. She would zip forward to a large skunk cabbage plant, and hover there for only a few seconds before becoming impatient.

Frederique thought: *If only it weren't for this bothersome shell, I could walk faster, maybe then she would talk to me instead of always buzzing about my slow pace.*

At that moment, Ruthie the Ruthless' patience wore out.

"You're too slow! Too slow! Why did I choose you as a partner? Some other creature will beat us and defeat the Dragon first."

So *it's true*, Frederique thought, and began digging a hole in the mud while Ruthie was busy ranting. *No one will be my friend because of this awful shell.*

His claws scooped away the cool, dark earth. It seemed his safe escape was always with him. When Ruthie finally stopped to take a breath, Frederique was gone.

"Hello? Turtle, are you there? Hello? Hello?" Ruthie called out. She would never admit it out loud, but she was quite afraid to be alone. "I am truly ruthless," she mourned.

Frederique could hear Ruthie's shrill pleas above. He could feel the silence below. Finally, Ruthie's calls stopped.

She's gone, he thought. *I will go home*

*now, and pretend like none of this
ever happened.*

   As he dug himself out of the mud, he
heard a rowdy rustling in the grasses
below him. To his surprise, he saw Ruthie
was still there, perched on a tree branch
intently watching whatever was causing
the ruckus. Frederique slowly crept
forward and peered through a tangle of
thickets. Down near the bank, he saw a
black and white furry monster plundering
a nest of recently lain turtle eggs,
devouring them one by one like flies.

6

The Ornery Skunk

Oh dear. The parents will be crushed.
But what can I do? he thought. I am as
useful as a rock, immobile and helpless,
Wait, like a rock. That could do!

"Ruthie! Ruthie!" he hissed.

"You? Where did you—"

"That monster, I've heard legends,
the Pondsfolk call it a skunk. Please go
distract it. It's destroying that turtle nest.
I'll try to save the eggs," said Frederique.

Ruthie dived down toward the skunk,
stopping right at the tip of its nose, and
hovering in front of its face.

"I can't seee!" the monster growled and swatted her away. She shook it off.

"Ok, let's try a different tactic," said Ruthie.

She buzzed rapidly in every direction, disorienting the skunk before jabbing him on his back where he couldn't reach her.

"Enough!" the skunk shouted, and he turned away from the nest to defend himself from her attacks.

At that moment, Frederique slid down the embankment toward the nest. He dug his claws into the mud, skidded to a stop just before the eggs and rested his shell over the nest, careful to leverage his weight so as to not crush the whole clutch.

The skunk had had enough of Ruthie's relentless attacks. "You measly sockeye! You dirty den of foxes!" he shouted.

24

He whacked her with his tail, this time leaving her a little dazed. The skunk turned back to his meal to find Frederique sitting there—afraid but resolute.

"Move! I was here first," said the skunk, now stomping his paws into the earth.

"No!" shouted Frederique.

"Fine then," said the skunk.

And the skunk began pushing Frederique, trying to topple him off of the eggs, but it didn't work. No matter the maneuver, Frederique would not budge. His shell was so heavy it was like a large stone.

Finally, the skunk turned around.

At last the terror is over, Frederique thought.

But the hungry skunk had one more trick.

He did a handstand, lifted up his tail, and sprayed a cloud of noxious fumes.

"Quick," Frederique shouted to Ruthie, "fly high into the trees!"

Frederique then pulled his neck deep into his spacious shell. The smell was bad, putrid, in fact. But the shelter of the shell lessened its effects and Frederique stayed there, unmoved, guarding the clutch of eggs.

7

A Honeysuckle Branch

"Hey, we're not such a bad team!" Ruthie zipped.

Frederique idled in a nearby pond chomping on some water lily; a new treat he had discovered since leaving the muck floor of his old pond.

Ruthie flew dizzily from flower to flower sucking in its nectar and renewing her spirits for their meeting with the Dragon.

"Where did you go earlier?" asked Ruthie.

"Oh, I just needed to slip away for a little break," he replied. He had hoped she had forgotten their quarrel.

"A break?" Ruthie started, "But you hardly move faster than a —" but she stopped herself.

Back home in South America, there were so many hummingbirds; each one brilliantly colored and even faster and feistier than her. But she was invisible, nothing special, not worth anyone's notice. Yet here was this turtle who had noticed her when she was muddied and defeated by the storm.

"Frederique, I'm sorry, so sorry, for losing my temper with you earlier. You didn't deserve that."

"It's ok," he said, "it wasn't unexpected."

Frederique had now begun intently gorging on some milfoil he had found.

"Listen," said Ruthie, "I say we keep going and try to find the Dragon and defeat him before nightfall."

"I suppose. What's a dragon but a skunk with wings and scales—and fire! Besides, then you can go back home and not have to bother with me anymore," Frederique replied.

"Well, that sounds like an enthusiastic yes. Why are you so down? We just made a victorious rescue and it was your idea!"

8

The Singing Bullfrog

So their journey continued, Ruthie flew near to Frederique and shared many stories about South America, her large family, and the many monsters she came face to face with back home. Frederique, though not quite as talkative, told her some stories about what it was like living back in Turtlestein Pond, but he felt there wasn't much to tell and was afraid he was boring her.

Soon they came upon a large marsh and right in the middle on a nearly submerged tree trunk stood a bullfrog with his throat puffed out and his stringy green limbs theatrically raised in the air. He was singing an opera, though,

31

clearly, he was not professionally trained, as it was dreadful.

Ruthie flew high into the sky to survey their surroundings.

"There it is," she said, "the Dried River where the Dragon flies! It's just up the hill on the other side of this marsh. Quick, I'll get on your back and help guide us through as you swim across."

Frederique slowly glided into the water. It was quite muddy much like where he used to wallow, and it gave him a bad feeling. As they started to swim, the bullfrog suddenly stopped mid vibrato. He popped one eye open and glared down at the odd pair swimming so freely right through his encore performance!

"Yoou have distuuurbed my shoooooow!" the bullfrog belted. "Who do you think you are? Showing up unannounced, how rude!"

"Sorry to interrupt, it's just that we have important business to attend and need to cross straight away," said Frederique.

"Humph. You? Important? Ha!" He released his gut and let it droop, warts and all, over the stump.

"We are going to defeat the Dragon!" Ruthie chimed.

"What? I think not! I shall defend the Dragon and challenge you to a duel!" croaked the bullfrog. "I like that fellow, though we haven't met; but he keeps pesky critters like you in their place, crushing them so that I hardly ever have anyone disturb my shows."

He picked up his slimy belly in his hands and plopped down onto a trout waiting for him at the base of the stump.

"Wait," said Frederique. "I don't want to fight."

"Ha! Of course not. Silly turtle, do you really think you can defeat me? Bird, why don't you just fly across and leave this turtle behind, he will only slow you down. You're nothing but a snail in an oversized shell! A dirt muncher!"

Frederique sank into his shell.

"A coward. Go back home and hide," the bullfrog shouted.

"Stop!" said Ruthie. "We will joust against you, and I'll topple you right off your trout!"

"No Ruthie. He's right; I can't do such a thing. What am I thinking? I'll always be a cumbersome and useless turtle," said Frederique.

"Don't let this opera singing bully tell you who you are," said Ruthie. "I'm your friend. I know who you are. You are brave. You are quick thinking. With your shell, you rescued me and protected the eggs from that monstrous skunk. Rumor has it you even saved the Royal Catfish from a giant. You are exactly who you need to be."

She's absolutely right, he thought. *I can do this!*

Frederique emerged from his shell and started swimming furiously toward the bullfrog. Ruthie perched on top with her beak poised in an attack. The bullfrog whipped the trout with his sharpened reed.

"Arrrrgh!"

"Crroooooooaaak!"

The bullfrog tried to jab his reed into Frederique but it hit his shell so hard that it bounced back and sent the bullfrog flying into the air. A crow happened to be flying past and swooped down and caught the bullfrog in his beak. "Mmm, dinner and a show," said the crow, "now that's high-class entertainment!"

9

A New Friend

Ruthie and Frederique both stopped and stared at each other until they burst into laughter.

"I guess you're not so soft," laughed Ruthie.

"No," said Frederique, "it seems I have my own built-in suit of armor. And I guess you're not so ruthless. Thank you for your encouragement back there. I think I've needed to hear that for many years now."

"Well, I wasn't going to let some bullfrog bully my friend."

"Friends?" said Frederique.

Even with all the colorful stripes on his face, she could tell he was beaming.

"Yes, friends," she fluttered.

So they continued on their way and very soon made it to the Dried River. The air was somber and smelled of gas and smoke. The Dragon was lurking nearby.

"What are you doing here?" whispered a voice from behind. "This place is dangerous," said the voice again.

Frederique and Ruthie turned and faced a large creature covered from head to tail in thin sharp spikes. It was an old silver-backed porcupine with a soft white tuft of hair on top of her head. Her nose had a cut that was still bleeding and her paws hung limp and swollen.

"I didn't mean to frighten," said the porcupine, "I'm Quill. I tried, myself, to defeat the Dragon, but as you can see the Dragon defeated me." Quill held out her paws to show them.

"What happened?" said Ruthie.

"It seems I'm too slow and he crushed my hands as I tried to attack," said Quill, "I'm lucky it wasn't worse."

Frederique winced, "That's terrible."

"But how did you find yourself here?" asked Ruthie, "I've never known a porcupine to live on the island of San Juan."

"I journeyed from the North and across the waters. My family back home lost most of our food supply after one of the great forest fires. I had hoped that if I could save the Pondsfolk of the Royal Kingdom of the Ponds, in return, King Heron would let me harvest a store of bark and seeds to bring home to my family and all my grand porcupettes."

Frederique and Ruthie were not sure how to respond to all that Quill had faced.

"If you let me," Frederique said to Quill, "I can find some mud and cover your hands in it. The mud will help to cool the pain and when it dries will protect them from further injury."

"That is very kind, yes, thank you," said Quill.

10

The Plan

Frederique went searching and found a cool mixture of mud and clay that he slowly began to scoop into his claws. He was saddened for Quill and worried. If Quill, being much larger and with built-in weaponry could not defeat the Dragon, then surely there was nothing that he or Ruthie could do to help.

The journey ends here, he thought. *But, where will Quill go? What about her family?*

Just then he heard an eruption of high-pitched laughter coming from the trees above.

"Teh hee hee hee," laughed two Douglas squirrels. They were Pine and Chickaree: a pair of siblings who had grown plump from stealing others' food.

"Teh hee hee hee, what a foolish turtle, doesn't even know what hit him!" laughed Chickaree.

"Seems you're as dense as your shell!" shouted Pine.

Frederique was confused. He looked around to see what they were talking about and saw a mound of acorns and pinecones lying around him. They had been throwing these at him the whole time, but he had not felt it in the slightest. And then he remembered, he had his own built-in suit of armor.

Maybe there is hope, he thought.

"Thanks," he yelled to the squirrels,

"you two are brilliant!" Pine and Chickaree were stunned.

"What are you talking about?" they shouted. "Shouldn't you be hiding in a pond somewhere?"

But Frederique was already on his way back to Quill and Ruthie with a plan forming in his mind.

"What a strange and curious turtle," said the squirrels.

Frederique told Quill and Ruthie his plan as he rubbed the mud and clay mixture gently over Quill's paws.

"I heard the Dragon has a weak spot," said Ruthie. "One of the robins said that she had once seen a dragon stopped in its destructive path when its underbelly was pierced."

"It's true," said Quill, "I've heard legends that the quill from an old porcupine can defeat a dragon, that's why I thought I stood a chance. Here, I want you to take my strongest and sharpest spike, it's on my left side tucked behind my arm."

Frederique slowly removed the spike, it looked threatening, rather large for a creature of even his size.

"You are very brave, Frederique," said Quill.

Then they heard a loud rumbling coming from down the path of the Dried River. Billows of dust began to swarm and the stones on the ground began to rattle.

"And you are not alone!" shouted Ruthie.

But Frederique couldn't hear her over the Dragon's roar or over the fear that pounded through his shell.

11

The Drag Racing Dragon

Frederique moved into the Dried River
with Quill's strongest spike in his hands.
It was almost dusk now and Frederique
could see the eyes of creatures big and
small watching him and waiting under
safe cover on either side.

Then, Quill gave the signal and Ruthie
led the way for a mass of birds: robins,
warblers, gulls, and mallards, and a few
early rising owls. They collected together
and formed a wall across the Dried River.
Ruthie hovered in front and stared down
the Dragon charging right toward her, and
the birds, and her friend, Frederique.

Lightning-like fire glared from its two

eyes and black smoke curled out from its nose. Its tail swerved in a zig zag, its body was bright red with black stripes and strange sounds blared from its stomach. Frederique desperately wanted to escape and hide in the mud, just disappear and forget it all, it would be so easy. But the lonesome thought of hiding in his shell terrified him even more, and now others depended on him too, so he stood his ground.

Then, he heard the Dragon let off a deafening squeal as it suddenly slowed at the sight of the birds, this was Frederique's signal. He tucked his body into his shell and held out Quill's spike at an angle positioned just so. The Dragon's rubber belly rolled directly over him and he could feel the pressure, like a boulder being stacked upon a pebble. He could hardly breathe but held tightly to the spike which pierced through the dark tar underside of the Dragon and left

Frederique's claws.

There was a loud hissing sound like the wind of an angry snake slithering across a meadow. Frederique stayed in his shell, not knowing whether he was alive or dead.

But then it seemed the whole kingdom erupted into a relieved chorus of chirrups and squeaks and whistles. Frederique came out of his shell and saw the body of the Dragon above him. He slowly moved out into the open and with the smoke and dust cleared, he saw that it was true. The Dragon had been stopped, the animals had been saved!

12

The Favor of King Heron

Ruthie came and perched on the edge of Frederique's shell.

"You did it Frederique! We did it!" sang Ruthie.

All at once the cheering stopped and was replaced with the sort of silence reserved for the first winter snow.

"Look up," Ruthie whispered.

There above them was the black silhouette of a bird unlike any other, it was long and slender, and it moved toward them like a quiet stream in the sky. King Heron landed in the middle

of the throng of animals. He stood unmoving like a great oak tree and peered down at Frederique and Ruthie.

"Well," King Heron said at last, "when I issued my proclamation, I never imagined that the creatures to defeat the Dragon would be a turtle and a hummingbird. I've been watching the two of you make your journey. You are both inventive and extremely brave. Now, what may I do for each of you as a thank you on behalf of the Pondsfolk?"

Neither answered.

"You first, Ruthie the Ruthless," said the king.

Ruthie looked around and saw that she was surrounded by friends and an assortment of birds who had trusted her, and who had thought she was special. Most importantly, she saw Frederique.

"I believe, King Heron that I have already found what it was I was truly seeking. I only ask you allow me to continue to travel here not only on my migration each year, but whenever I may choose to visit my dear friends."

"Done," said King Heron. "You are welcome whenever you would like for as long as you desire."

"And you, curious turtle, there must be something I can offer you, Frederique. It can't always be easy being a turtle."

"You are correct, King Heron, it is not always easy being a turtle, especially one with such a shell, but it is exactly who I am meant to be and I would not change a thing," answered Frederique.

Frederique looked at the animals all waiting to see what he would think to ask of King Heron, and he noticed

Quill sitting there. She was smiling at Frederique, but she looked homesick and deeply tired.

"King Heron, my request is on behalf of my friend, Quill. Allow her to harvest as much bark and seeds as she needs and bring it home to her family affected by the forest fires. Without her or any of my friends, we would not have been able to defeat the Dragon."

The forest of animals broke into hoots and trills of applause.

"Done," said King Heron. "However, I would like to add something to your request. I have witnessed the fire's sweeping hunger and have seen the charred and barren land left behind. I've watched the families of animals searching for a new home. Therefore, I will send a band of Pondsfolk to help bring even more stores of food as well as tree saplings to restore the forested lands once more."

The Pondsfolk all started jabbering and volunteering at once.

"We can gather materials and weave baskets to carry supplies," said some of the birds.

"I could carry an especially large load on top of my shell," said Frederique.

"I can protect them as they travel," said Ruthie.

"Thank you," Quill whispered to Frederique.

"And for their bravery," declared King Heron, "and for learning that by befriending one's true self and being a friend to others, all manner of foes can be defeated; may this hummingbird and this turtle now be known as Ruthie the Remarkable and Sir Frederique von Turtlestein."

Epilogue

A Brave Turtle

Now, if you ever make your own journey to the islands of San Juan and find yourself in the Royal Kingdom of the Ponds, then you may see for yourself an elusive fox darting like a ray of sun through shaded woods.

Or glimpse the black tips of a pod of orcas moseying through the waters, hinting at a whole other world beneath you.

You might see a hummingbird perched on a tree branch, so small and still, it looks like a stubborn leaf that refused to fall.

Or you may even see a brave, old red-eared slider turtle with an incredibly large shell perched on a rock; his neck stretched out as far as he can reach to the early morning sun.

THE END

Meet the Author

Amanda Geers earned a BA in English: Creative Writing with an emphasis in poetry at Seattle Pacific University.

A mom to both humans and animals, she nourishes her soul through dance, communing with nature, and following her writing dreams. She lives in a cabin like home in the woods of Sammamish, WA. You can follow her journey at amandageers.com.

Meet the Illustrator

Vincent Stevens is an artist and accountant finding meaning in both artistic impressions and precision. He has won many art contests and his oil painting of the White River in AZ was exhibited in a world tour.

He has four beautiful children and now lives in Woodinville, WA with his high school sweetheart, two alpacas, and their herd of adopted senior shelties.

Did you love the story?

Help Sir Frederique & Ruthie
continue their journey
by leaving a review!

Amazon· https://amzn.to/3HAEvjb

Goodreads· https://bit.ly/3nur7oZ

Thank you! Sincerely,

CPSIA information can be obtained
at www.ICGtesting.com
Printed in the USA
BVHW051340230921
617330BV00006B/169